YOU WILL GO FAR

YOU WILL GO FAR

WORDS AND ILLUSTRATIONS BY
JENNY KEMPE

Andrews McMeel
Publishing

Kansas City · Sydney · London

Andrews McMeel Publishing, LLC
an Andrews McMeel Universal company
1130 Walnut Street, Kansas City, Missouri 64106

www.andrewsmcmeel.com

15 16 17 18 19 SBD 10 9 8 7 6 5 4 3 2 1

ISBN: 978-1-4494-6009-9
Library of Congress Control Number: 2014941959

Jenny Kempe
69 Harbord Street, London, SW6 6PL, UK
E: jenny@jennykempe.com, www.jennykempe.com

ATTENTION: SCHOOLS AND BUSINESSES

Andrews McMeel books are available at quantity discounts with bulk purchase for educational, business, or sales promotional use. For information, please e-mail the Andrews McMeel Publishing Special Sales Department: specialsales@amuniversal.com.

CONGRATULATIONS!

To: _Payton_

From: _Tatie ♥_

CONGRATULATIONS!

You are a star, you truly are!

IDEAS FOR LIFE

☐ Graduate
☐ Travel the World
☐ Make art (movies/music?)
☐ Make millions
☐ Build igloo
☐ Find True Love ❤
☐ Save Planet
☐ Nobel prize?
☐ _____
☐ _____
☐ _____
☐ _____

Set some goals and spread your wings.

You're off to do remarkable things.

See the world from sea to shore.

Pack your stuff and go explore!

It's what you want
that you need to know.

Don't hesitate, don't doubt.
Take the first step — just go.

Some days may be glum and dreary . . .

others quite extraordinary!

Perhaps you jump out of bed
and race right ahead.

Perhaps you need a bit of time.
Sitting still is not a crime.

Some go fast, and some go slow.
Some fly high, and some fly low.

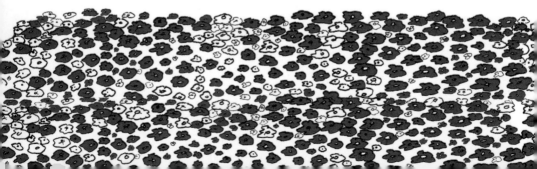

Some go fast, and some go slow.
Some fly high, and some fly low.

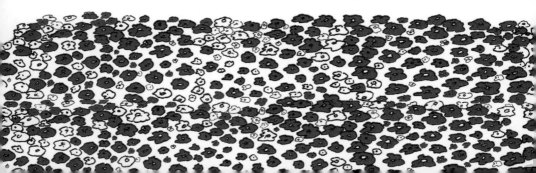

Whichever way you take,
however well you steer,
speed bumps can and will appear.

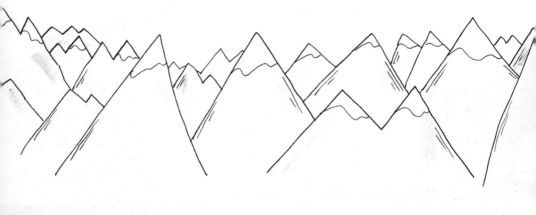

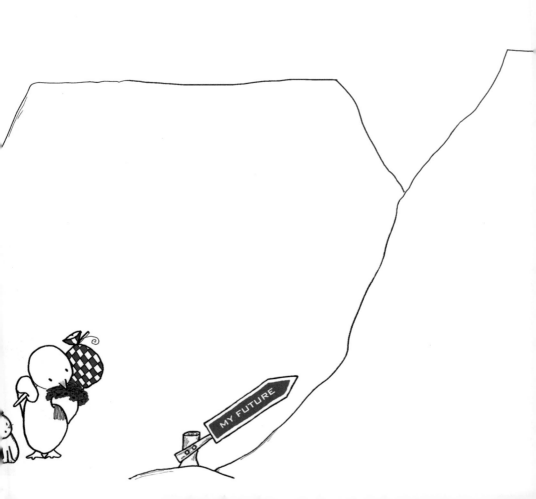

Trials and tribulations
will test your character
and patience.

MY FUTURE

But none of those
will hold you back.

You're a bright-shining star;
you'll be right back on track.

You'll make new acquaintances.

Some you like, and some you don't.

Some you'll love,

and some you won't.

There are those who are nice,
and there are those who are not.
Be polite and gracious to the whole lot.

Respect both beast and man.

Be kind, because you can.

Learn to take these in your stride:
Misfortune, pain, and wounded pride.

Talk about your feelings, if they're true.

Others will know
what you're going through.

If you find yourself
in a clique,

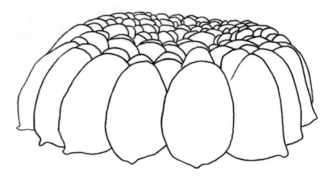

keep in mind you are
perfectly unique.

Don't think it's a defeat . . .

if you can't immediately find your feet.

It can tear your heart in tatters—
thinking of your life,
and of what really matters.

You may hit a wall;
unable to get
anywhere at all.

Clouded by doubt and fears,
you move around in circles
until your vision clears.

Until then, keep it Zen.

Stay in the now.

Inhale, exhale,
that's how.

Sooner or later,
the answers will come.

(If not all, then some.)

Astronauts
Wanted

Finding stimulation
will help your motivation.

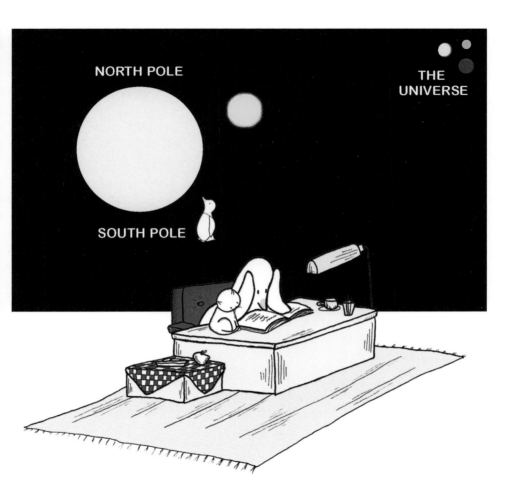

And if you also learn to play,
you're sure to have a better day.

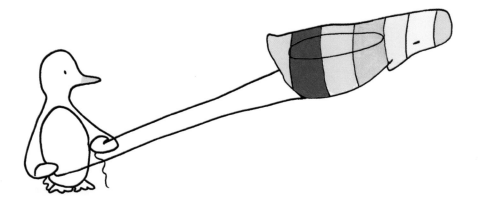

Seek the safe, or the thrilling,
whatever you find fulfilling.

Be laid-back, chilled, and free . . .

happy to just hang out and be.

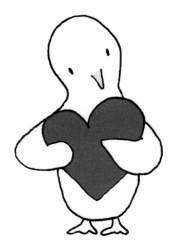

Know that you are
an incredible,
amazing creation.

Worthy of love and adoration.

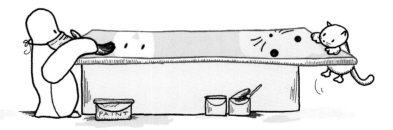

One way or other,
you will light your spark
and make your mark.

The best that you can be:
Plain and simple
for everyone to see.

Wherever you go,
whatever you choose to do,
there will be an adventure waiting

JUST FOR YOU.

GOOD
LUCK!